opqrstuvwxyz

12|81

First American Edition
Copyright © 1984 by John Burningham
All rights reserved
Published in 1984 by The Viking Press
40 West 23rd Street, New York, New York 10010
Published in Great Britain by Walker Books Ltd.
Printed in Italy
1 2 3 4 5 88 87 86 85 84
ISBN 0-670-65016-1
Library of Congress catalog card number: 83-25981
(CIP data available)

skip trip

John Burningham

THE VIKING PRESS
NEW YORK

hop

kick

throw

catch

slip

trip

bounce

skip

swing

drop

pull

push

run

jump

dive

slump

abcdefghijklm